THE BIG CRUNCH and THE FIX

A Political Vision for Healing America's Wounds Inflicted by Our Malignant Economic & Social Policies

By

H. Lewis Smith

This book is for all American citizens who are
concerned and anxious about our current
Executive and Legislative branches of
government, and other environmental,
economic, and social issues.

TABLE OF CONTENTS

SECTION 1

THE
BIG CRUNCH

INTRODUCTION

I am an apprehensive and concerned American citizen. I usually write novels, but this book is not fictional; unfortunately, it is real. Our democratic political system is in a state of disarray and stagnation. Entrenched career politicians have become arrogant, power-hungry, and more concerned about themselves than their constituents. The executive and legislative branches of government are at war with each other, and the rhetoric is disgusting and appalling. Due to unequal trade balances, the United States has become a debtor nation, and we are increasing that debt by approximately $1 trillion each year. Democracy and capitalism are the world's best systems, but our platform has significant flaws. If we do not make some changes, the United States will lose its ranking as the world's largest economy and the best, most efficient, and fair governmental system. Failure to make some changes will result in the *'Big Crunch.'* We can correct these issues by implementing *'The Fix,'* and by effecting these changes, we will maintain our world economic and legislative status, and Americans can be proud once again.

I am not a politician or an economist. I am a registered Republican because I cannot vote in our state primaries as an independent, but I do not consider myself a

Republican or Democrat. I am a moderate fiscal conservative and a social progressive. My political affiliation would probably fall under the heading of "*none*." I am not a communist, nationalist, or socialist, nor am I a pacifist. Still, I believe most wars initiated in the later 20th century and early 21st century by America were nothing short of absurdity and madness. I am independent and dislike any organization or group telling me what I should believe, who I should support, or how I should vote or conduct my life. I realize that the job of a political party is to promote a candidate and their platform, but I make my decision based upon what the candidates say and support.

I believe in free speech, religious freedom, nonviolent protest, freedom of movement, and freedom to determine your own destiny; however, I do not support the right for everyone to bear arms. I can see the necessity for such a provision in 1776, but not in 2020. Private ownership of semi-automatic firearms is nothing short of insanity. They are for killing only and nothing else.

Beginning with the Korean War, I became uncomfortable with our political system, government ethics, and values. I am a capitalist, but the deregulations associated with Neo-liberal capitalism in the 20th century have created many unintended consequences such as giant money center banks, massive corporations, and unfair and unequal wealth distribution. Our monetary and political policies, although capitalist and democratic, have become corrupt, teeming with greed, and controlled mostly by an aristocratic minority interested only in themselves, their wealth, and the desire to be re-elected.

I am also concerned about the damage and pollution of our environment, resulting in climate change and contamination of our oceans, waterways, and landscape. The Trump administration has executed some deregulations, which will worsen the problems.

If we don't make some changes soon, I believe our citizens will revolt in some manner, and the correction may be more drastic than necessary with possible tragic unintended consequences. I propose '*The Fix*' as a way to implement change that I believe will benefit everyone.

HISTORICAL AND RECENT EVENTS

Adolf Hitler, the megalomaniacal Chancellor/ Dictator/Fuehrer of Germany, started World War II. His goal was to control and enslave the population of Europe and Russia, and ethnically cleanse the Aryan population by exterminating the Jews. If the United States had not entered the war, there is a strong probability everyone in Europe would now be speaking German, all aristocrats and intelligentsia would've been murdered, and the superior (Hitler's opinion) Aryan populace would have enslaved and now be controlling the entire area. The world should be grateful for the leadership of Dwight D. Eisenhower and the willingness of the Allied forces to engage and eventually win the war against a well-trained, motivated, and equipped German army.

The Korean War was controversial, and many questioned the need for that conflict. Looking at the situation today in North Korea, you know we did not win that war. North Korea is a communist nation, and the dictator's rhetoric is anything but positive toward the United States and other democratic countries.

I followed the Vietnamese war closely, and I believed that somehow, our political leaders were either misinformed, victims of bad advice, or motivated by some political or economic goal — possibly a combination of all the above. Vietnam was a communist nation when we invaded it. After all the death, destruction, war injuries, and spending the equivalent of $1 trillion in today's money, Vietnam is still a communist nation. Millions of Americans objected and protested the war, creating a disturbing and distressing period in our history. I think their concerns and objections were valid.

President Richard Nixon probably did nothing that other high-level politicians have not done, except he got caught. I believe that had Nixon been truthful, American citizens would have forgiven him, and he could have finished his presidential term. Nixon was so paranoid, distrustful, and fearful of losing power that he surrounded himself with enablers and facilitators and considered himself almost invincible. He was mistaken. I sometimes wonder how we could have been duped and deceived (I voted for Nixon) by such an obfuscator of the truth. I remember the other choice was not very impressive. I had some direct contact with one of his brothers and his mother. Hannah Nixon was a remarkable and outstanding lady, but his brother not very notable. I was invited to the Nixon second inauguration and had some indirect contact with the president – I was not impressed and never had any significant respect or admiration for him. The Watergate scandal in which the tapes revealed that Nixon knew about and approved the break-in resulted in his impending impeachment. He resigned as president, becoming the only American president to resign from office voluntarily.

Gerald Ford was appointed president after the resignation of Richard Nixon, and I remember little about his presidency. I have always considered him almost a nonentity – a stand-in for the next real thing.

President Jimmy Carter was a peanut farmer and Governor of Georgia, and possibly very good at both, but as President, he seemed out of his league. I remember interest rates being outrageously high during most of his term in office, and his mishandling of the Iranian hostage crisis was tragic. Some of it may not have been his fault, but he was sitting at the head of the table, and as President Truman once said, "The buck stops here."

Although I voted for him, I had only modest respect for Ronald Reagan. His manipulation of the release of the American prisoners in Iran until after he was sworn in as President was outrageous, disgraceful, and shameful. If that wasn't *quid pro quo,* then I have been misinformed. His revamping of the tax code helped to set the stage for the incredible disparity between the super-wealthy and the rest of us, and his closing of our mental health facilities was a tragic mistake. The system was being misused and abused, but the closure of those facilities was a significant factor in our current homelessness problem and the mental health issues associated with it. Correction of the problems and keeping the facilities open would have been a much better choice.

During President George HW Bush's era, the United States had depleted many of its known oil reserves and was dependent upon Middle East oil. Saddam Hussein's invasion of Kuwait presented a dilemma. Bush decided to liberate Kuwait. Fortunately, almost the entire war against Iraq was conducted by air, and American troop casualties were minimal. Again, his decision to end the war when the forces retreated into Iraq was and continues to be controversial. I probably would have made a different decision, but perhaps there were some issues I am not aware of.

I never trusted either of the Clintons, just too many strange deals, relationships, and unusual personal connections. President Clinton had one significant flaw; his zipper was open more frequently than necessary for emptying his bladder. Special forces had Osama bin Laden in their crosshairs, and Clinton was so preoccupied with the impeachment process and other personal matters that he failed to give the go-ahead to pull the trigger. The consequences of that failure were enormous. Somehow along the way, the Clintons managed to amass a wealth of approximately $45 million. When Hillary Clinton was a senator and later Secretary of State, they secured donations of over $2 billion for the Clinton foundation from US corporations, foreign governments, foreign corporations, political donors, and various other groups. Why would a foreign government or corporation donate funds to the Clinton foundation unless they wanted something in return? There have been many criticisms of the Clinton foundation, some possibly politically motivated, but others probably valid. Emails uncovered indicate that foreign governments and foreign corporations that donated to the Clinton Foundation received special treatment. Also, it must be challenging to acquire $45 million of wealth on the salary of a public servant.

Then came President George Bush, son of H.W., who signed a bill that prohibited Medicare from negotiating drug prices. Inexcusable! It was one of several reasons for the outrageous increase in the price of prescription drugs in the US. The contract expired during the Obama administration, and Obama signed it again. The money associated with super PACs and political donations by industrial groups is effective, and money works in high places. I will discuss this issue in more detail under *"The Fix."*

The Second Iraq War was so misguided, ill-advised, and unnecessary that I find it challenging to address. It was a nightmare of huge numbers of deaths, injury, and permanent disability to American troops and Iraqi citizens. Approximately 31,000 young men and women of our military sustained severe and often permanent injury, with many being single or multiple amputees. When Bush and Cheney declared war on Iraq, I said to myself, "They undoubtedly must know something that I don't; otherwise, this is insanity." As it turns out, they were no more knowledgeable than me, and oilman Cheney was very influential, and possibly the primary instigator, of that war. Saddam Hussein posed no credible threat at that time, and the second Iraqi war became a tragic strain on our foreign policy.

The 9/11 twin tower destruction in New York was probably not preventable, given the lax protection mechanisms we had in place. That terrorist attack obviously required a response, but declaring war on Afghanistan was not the answer, and besides, most of the perpetrators were originally from Saudi Arabia. It was a war we could not win for many reasons. If the populace of a hostile country is not on your side and the nation is mountainous and vast, and you are not prepared to wage a full-scale war of mass destruction, you probably are not going to win that war.

President Barack Obama conducted himself in a reasonably honorable manner and made some excellent decisions, especially while navigating the economic crisis of 2008 and 2009. Many of the restrictions, rules, regulations, and laws enacted were necessary, but some went too far and had unexpected and undesirable consequences. He did have the good judgment to issue some Executive Orders, which were admirable and needed, including the problem of workplace bias. But he also re-signed the bill forbidding Medicare negotiation of drug prices; what was he thinking, and why?

We are now nearing the end of the first term of the Trump presidency. Words escape me concerning his administration. There is no need; he tweets it almost daily. Donald Trump is a misguided embarrassment as a president, but he still has a significant number of die-hard supporters. One of my biggest concerns is he has no perception of how the government functions or what the role of the chief executive is. He is unable to focus on issues and discuss the pros and cons with his advisers and then make a reasonable decision. He is also entirely obsessed with downgrading and removing anyone in his administration who does not agree with and support everything he does and says. There has been a significant turnover of personnel in the Trump government, and I strongly suspect there are issues with obtaining capable and experienced people to fill the vacancies. Trump also frequently makes untrue statements, and when confronted later, he denies ever having made them. It would be fascinating to see a psychiatric evaluation of President Trump. However, if the Democratic nominee in 2020 is not a candidate, the public can identify with and proposes rational and reasonable solutions to our many problems, Trump may be reelected. That could have grave consequences for our country and many other nations.

I will be proposing ideas about how to initiate some changes and discuss them in the second section titled *"The Fix"* but first a discussion of specific problems with our government, economy, and social policies.

THE BICAMERAL LEGISLATURE

The US House of Representatives and Senate have many significant problems that are complex, deeply embedded, and multifaceted. One of the main issues concerns super PACs and swarms of advocates and lobbyists all controlled and financed by industrial sectors, banking, or other special groups, and that is only the tip of the iceberg.

The focus of the House and Senate has become misguided and redirected away from legislative bills for the benefit of American citizens. They have become victims of bribery (super PACs and lobbyists), which has motivated them to propose legislation that benefits only a single group or sector. Rather than negotiating and introducing new innovative legislation, they have become focused on themselves and their party, thus putting new, creative, and beneficial laws on the back burner. How can you be a competent or capable legislator when most of your time and energy is spent trying to block legislation, downgrading your opponent, or investigating a fellow elected leader?

The gerrymandering of territories for members of the House of Representatives is outrageous and absurd. Navigating a district is the equivalent of piecing together a complex jigsaw puzzle. This practice enables House Members to be reelected repeatedly.

Career legislators are the wrong choice. Once entrenched, they become arrogant, power-hungry, and focused internally rather than on their constituency. It is prevalent in both houses of the legislature. They will do whatever it takes to get reelected, damned be the consequences. Power and prestige are everything to them.

INFRASTRUCTURE and The ECONOMY

Much of our infrastructure is in disrepair and crumbling. Many of our roads, freeways, bridges, and overpasses are dangerous and unsafe. Many utility lines are above ground and vulnerable to high winds, fires, and floods. Broken power lines and the explosion of transmission control stations are a significant factor in devastating wildfires. PG&E on the West Coast and Paradise, California, are typical examples. The city of Paradise is now a heap of ashes and burned-out rubble – no longer a paradise, but hell on earth, and all from high winds and breakage of above-ground utility lines resulting in devastating fires.

Our railway passenger transportation system is antiquated and outdated. Many passenger trains do not have collision avoidance or hazard warning technology, which has been available for several years. Customer safety and wellbeing are not critical to them. In 2015 an Amtrak train from Washington DC traveling to New York City derailed in a suburb of Philadelphia, killing eight people and injuring 200 others. The engineer was moving the train at 102 mph around a curve where the recommended speed was 50 mph. If positive train control software had been on the train and sensors placed on the tracks, this pileup and the death and multiple injuries associated with it would not have happened. Why is it not mandatory that adequate safety measures be installed to protect the public?

Bridges, overpasses, waterways, and interstate freeways are mostly the financial responsibility of the federal government. The state or municipalities cannot afford to replace a crumbling bridge across a river, ocean waterway, or ravine. Many are dangerous, some have failed, and others are either unsafe or becoming so. At least two presidents have verbally addressed the problem, but again, nothing concrete (that's a pun) has happened

.

Our underground service delivery system is also antiquated, with water mains being a classic example. Breakage and leakage of the public water systems in Los Angeles are so common it does not make the news unless there is massive flooding, property damage, or disruption of traffic. A recent six-foot water main in Los Angeles ruptured with flooding and property damage. It was installed in 1914. Natural gas and other petroleum product pipelines are also common issues. You don't hear much about the sewage system or the underground water runoff and disposal systems, but they are also antiquated and problematic.

Our Neo-liberal capitalist economy has serious problems. One of the biggest issues is the grossly unequal distribution of wealth. The top 1% of the richest Americans control 40% of the wealth, and the other 99% control 60%. This unequal distribution of capital is not reasonable, but it isn't the end of the story – it's getting worse each year. We have almost reached the breaking point, and if we don't make some changes soon, some severe and unnecessary changes may happen.

OTHER ISSUES

Our macroeconomy is not in a good place. The last time we had a balanced budget was during the Clinton administration. The United States' current national debt is $22 trillion, and the gross domestic product for 2018 was $20.5 trillion. If our annual budget deficit continues to increase at the current rate, in ten years, we will have difficulty paying the interest, let alone the principal. To liquidate our maturing notes and bonds, we sell new ones to pay off the old. That is the equivalent of taking out a personal loan to make your mortgage payment. President Trump told us that by lowering the taxes on the wealthy and corporations, the economy would expand, and we would collect more tax revenues. Pie-in-the-sky promises are always a charade. Politicians frequently make similar assurances to justify reducing taxes on the super-wealthy or corporations.

Our tax system is unfair, unjust, and riddled with tax loopholes that benefit big business, the super-wealthy, and other special interest groups. Probably one of the many reasons Donald Trump refuses to release his tax returns is that he pays little or no taxes. One other possibility is that his wealth numbers released to the public are exaggerated, and the correct figures are much less. If the actual figures were released, he might find it necessary to *"get out of Dodge"* to avoid the debris hurled at him. Our tax system must be revised, rewritten, and made more equitable for everyone.

Our medical delivery system is unsustainable and almost terminal. We have 80 million people in the US who have no medical insurance or are grossly underinsured. As a result, we pay very high monthly premiums for coverage, and many policies have significant deductibles. Many young and healthy citizens are not purchasing insurance. Bernie Sanders, a Democratic presidential candidate for 2020, is proposing free Medicare for all and says they will pay the cost of $1.4 trillion by increasing taxes on the wealthy and corporations. The middle class would not have a tax increase. That is so much B-S I become nauseated just thinking about it. It is impossible to collect $1.4 trillion by raising taxes on the wealthy and corporations. In addition, several insurance companies would be put out of business, and thousands of their employees would be out of work. To implement such a program in a short timeframe reeks of stupidity and foolishness.

Our federal and local prison systems are overcrowded, antiquated, inadequately funded, and fostered by some laws and statutes which are embarrassing and brutal. Becoming the victim of addiction to an opioid, or marijuana, should not be a felony; it is a medical problem. To incarcerate a teenager for becoming addicted to OxyContin is the equivalent of convicting an innocent person for murder. Those who transport and sell those substances illegally for profit are an entirely different matter – they should be held accountable.

The appointment of federal judges and Supreme Court justices is entirely politicized. Selecting a judge based upon his or her political or religious affiliation is not appropriate. It should be based upon their record, experience, and proven ability to make reasonable and rational evidence-based decisions.

Our voting system is antiquated and outdated. Why must we continue to ignore and disregard technological progress when it is readily available and affordable? Some changes must happen.

Corruption and bribery involving public officials are much more common than most of us realize. It is being hidden and buried under the rug. We could be on the threshold of a limited fix, it will take time, but it is possible.

One of the most perplexing and disturbing problems is homelessness, poverty, and slums. If you drive to downtown Los Angeles, you confront another world of addiction, mental health issues, poverty, disease, rodents, fecal matter, homelessness, and hopelessness. If you drive through some regions of Southeast Los Angeles, you see a similar but slightly less extreme, degrading, and deteriorating community. It is disturbing, frightening, and depressing. How can this happen in a modern democratic society such as ours? These are not inherently bad people, they just have been dealt a lousy hand, and they need our help. The rescue rate will never be 100%, but there is a partial solution. It will not be easy or quick, and it will cost some money. We must assist our fellow citizens.

The military-industrial complex first brought to our attention by President Dwight Eisenhower, has become a monster money pit. Our military expenditure is the equivalent of the military budget of the next 75 countries combined! We believe we are the protector and guardian of the entire planet and disburse our military weapons, ships, aircraft, and troops accordingly. That concept may have been a good idea and possibly necessary following World War II, but at this time, it is unnecessary. We backed ourselves into a rut by creating a non-militarized zone in Korea and agreeing to protect it, and we are probably stuck with that obligation, at least, for now. Future wars, except those by small underdeveloped nations, are not going to be fought on the ground by foot soldiers; they will be conducted in the air and on the seas. Our military force could and should be reduced. Most future wars will also be of short duration. Our extensive and often nearly obsolete military equipment and supplies are a significant financial burden and entirely unnecessary. Reducing the vast stockpiles of military equipment should be a priority.

The size of our atomic arsenal is another issue of enormous concern, as it should be, and must eventually be significantly dismantled; otherwise, our future could be bleak, dark, dreary, and possibly lifeless.

Immigration and undocumented immigrants are a sensitive and challenging problem to solve. There were 11.4 million undocumented immigrants in the United States in 2019. Many are from Mexico and Central America, but significant numbers are from Asia and several other countries scattered around the globe. Illegal border crossings have decreased in the past 2-3 years, but illegal residents have increased. Fewer are coming, but more are staying. The situation is problematic and difficult to control. Some states and municipalities have become safe havens and passed ordinances that restrict law enforcement in attempting their arrest and deportation. Many of the undocumented are decent, honest, productive, and law-abiding members of the community, yet we continue to threaten them and search for ways to arrest and deport them. President Trump has repeatedly said, "There are a lot of bad people trying to cross our borders illegally." He may be right to some degree, but the "bad people" are the minority, not the majority, and his focus has been on that minority. We are a nation of immigrants, and we must deal with this issue. It is embarrassing to live in a country with several million undocumented immigrants who are often abused, misused, and living in fear and have no legal rights. There is a solution, but it will require a change in attitude and approach. We should not demonize those who are honest and decent, hard-working people. The answer will require a shift in perspective and approach. We must do the right thing.

The final issue is student loan debt. To have an entire generation of young people beginning their lives saddled with an enormous debt is inconceivable and ludicrous. The current student debt is $1.47 trillion. You may not be young and in debt, but your children or grandchildren might be victims. It is a vital issue that has recently garnered much attention, and several journalists have written extensive articles concerning the problem. Addressing this issue is critical.

This concludes my outline of the many significant issues, but don't be discouraged or depressed – a fix is possible. You probably will not agree with all of my recommendations, but I anticipate mostly positive support and approval. Many people I meet, including Democrats, Republicans, Independents, and *Nones*, have similar feelings of anxiety, frustration, and concern.

Democracy and capitalism are the best government and economic systems, but we have failed to modernize or adapt to a global economy, technological advances, or progressive social policies. We are incredibly fortunate to live in a nation that permits freedom of thought and speech and the ability to choose and decide your future. Unfortunately, those original concepts have been pushed aside and replaced by greed and control by major corporations and banking establishments. American citizens must assert themselves and reaffirm those rights granted us by our forefathers who wrote the Constitution and Bill of Rights.

Some changes that will benefit everyone, not just the super-wealthy or large corporations, are necessary. I am not trying to control or dictate to you. I just want to get your attention and help in improving our government, our economic system, and overall well-being. I hope to interest you in participating in a rational problem-solving experience called "The Fix."

30

SECTION II

THE FIX

PROPOSALS AND DISCUSSION

To create change in a democracy, it is not necessary to participate in a stampede. When faced with significant issues, our government tends to become polarized, which is a serious issue with our current legislative and executive branches. It is quick and easy to become hostile and combative and refuse to negotiate, but it is counterproductive. And injecting religious views into the political arena further exacerbates hostilities, leading to increased polarity resulting in stagnation.

Trying to move to the center and not the radical periphery is a better choice. Debate, negotiate, exchange ideas, and become positive rather than negative. If we do not elect a new generation of legislative and executive leaders, we will probably remain stuck in our current rut of polarization and failure to progress. The cost of radical change would be significant, and the wealth tax proposed could not possibly support the programs. We need change, but a drastic or fundamental alteration could have serious consequences. If we expand our national debt more rapidly than we presently are, *"The Big Crunch"* will occur sooner than later. A 3-5 year breathing span may be necessary to make some of the suggested changes.

It is not necessary to drain a swamp by opening all the floodgates simultaneously; open one lock at a time and let it trickle away slowly but surely. Our only chance to effect reasonable, rational, and well thought out change is to walk cautiously toward some new goals, not race around the track weaving and dodging to avoid hazards. A turtle is a much better choice than a rabbit.

The first obstacle to change is the legislature and the executive branches. Unless we elect a new generation of legislators and executives, the changes proposed will probably never happen. Most voters are over the age of 50, and the youth can protest, wave their banners, and scream into the megaphones, and nothing will change unless they vote. Not just one of them; it must be all of them. Very few in our younger generation are racist, biased, bigoted, or predisposed to blocking change and progress. They do tend to be impatient, and that can be good or bad. Severely agitated people are frequently careless and impulsive, which is not the best approach. Fortunately, we live in a democratic society that permits change without violence. If you stick a gun in my face, I'm going to fight like hell, but if you offer me an ice cream bar, I'll probably smile and welcome you inside.

The 2020 Democratic presidential debates were exciting and informative but depressing at the same time. Only two candidates consistently proposed change, that seemed reasonable and rational. The debates were also encouraging because I witnessed the beginning of something exciting and new, the younger generation. They seem focused, intelligent, filled with energy, and eager to tackle life.

I know a young man in his late 20s who has just completed his MBA and become a wage earner for the first time. He seems satisfied with his present work environment, and I asked him what his future goal was, and without hesitation, he said, "I'm going to be the CEO." The best news of all, he has no student loan debt. We need motivated and inspiring leaders, not timid followers. Be vocal and assert yourselves and your ideas.

In conclusion, we do not have an immediate crisis, but we have a major political and economic problem that will become *A Big Crunch* soon unless we affect change. We do not need to make an immediate or careless right or left turn. If we stay in the middle-of-the-road, and work hard for change, we will all reap the benefits.

The next chapters are devoted to change, advancement, and innovation, and we will start with the executive branch and work our way down the list.

THE EXECUTIVE BRANCH

It would be wonderful to feel proud, positive, and honored to discuss our recent executive leaders, but, unfortunately, that is not true. Both political parties seem to have become radicalized – the Democratic Party is moving to the left, and the Republican Party has moved to the right. There is a middle ground, which is the better platform, but how do you create it? One possible solution is a third political party, however that could be very problematic. The last time we had a third party (Tea Party), it was even farther to the right than the Republican Party. Most third-party systems are cumbersome, difficult to control, and challenging to obtain a consensus. One other method would be to create a third grouping of *Independents* to encourage like-minded thinkers to run for political office but still caucus with one of the two political parties. I think it unlikely that an Independent presidential candidate could get elected within the next decade.

A new generation of executive leaders is the answer, and it should be sooner than later. We need to make some changes now. They may only be baby steps, but, at least, they will be steps, and hopefully, in the right direction.

Article II Section I of the U.S. Constitution established the electoral college. If given a chance, many people would vote to abolish it, but that might be a mistake. The East Coast and West Coast would then elect the president, and middle America would have little or no voice.

The 22nd Amendment states that no person shall occupy the office of president or vice president for more than two four-year terms. That amendment has had some unintended consequences: it encourages a president to spend significant time and energy during the first term trying to get reelected. It is expensive, time-consuming, and disruptive, and makes the chief executive vulnerable to the whims of the major contributors. It's a part of the philosophy of 'you support me, and I will fund you.' To rid our political system of such a waste of time, we should sponsor a constitutional amendment that provides for a single presidential term of six years, which would change everything. I do not see any downside and a significant upside.

A law eliminating super PACs and donations by special groups or organizations is essential. Individual contributions should be the only alternative. Until that bill is passed, the new generation candidates must be strongly urged to refuse donations from any super PAC, industrial group, big corporation, or organization. Several Democratic candidates for president in 2020 have set the gold standard by doing mostly just that. They should be applauded for this extraordinary step forward.

The next generation, which includes candidates in their late 30s, 40s, or 50s, will be the solution. A 75-year-old president is probably not going to welcome much change unless it is radical change. In other words, socialism. It is not necessary to dismantle our current democratic or capitalist system. We need only to modify it and make it more applicable to our modern era and benefit everyone. Just reshuffle the cards, more equitably. Don't discard the entire deck.

THE LEGISLATIVE BRANCH

We have a bicameral legislative system consisting of the House of Representatives and the Senate. Collectively they are known as the National Legislature. The House of Representatives is called the lower house, and the Senate is known as the upper chamber.

There are no term limits for members of the House of Representatives. The house is composed of congressional districts that are allocated to each of the 50 states based upon population. The total number of voting members is 435. Several states have only one representative, and the state of California has 53. All federal bills must originate in the House of Representatives and, when approved, are then sent to the Senate for approval or modification and then presented to the President for his consideration. All legislative bills relating to revenue must originate in the House of Representatives.

It's a great system, and we should be proud that our founders conceived and wrote such a fair and equitable system, while most other nations were stagnating in a monarchal system, which gave complete and total power to one person – no executive order needed; do what I say and do it now.

The lower house system has two flaws, one is no term limits, and the other is the gerrymandering of congressional districts. The boundaries of the districts are drawn in such a way that it is challenging to unseat an incumbent. Mapping the boundaries of the congressional districts is a state, not a federal issue. District boundaries should be done by appointed members of a panel, not a political party. They should draw those boundaries more reasonably and logically. Trying to navigate your way through a gerrymandered congressional district in California is like trying to find your way out of a corn maze.

The most crucial issue is term limits. We must enact them, but to accomplish that, we must elect some new members to the House. We must amend the Constitution for a limit of five two-year terms. Since all revenue bills originate in The House, we must also elect some new money managers. As a wise person once said,

"Out with the old, and in with the new."

The United States Senate is known as the upper chamber and consists of two elected members from each of the 50 States. Elected members serve a six-year term. The terms are staggered so that one-third of the members are elected every two years. There are no term limits, and the Senate has some unique responsibilities – they can originate and pass bills, or ratify or modify proposals submitted by the House of Representatives. They also have the authority to investigate and or conduct the trial of the president or other federal employees who have been impeached by the house. In the impeachment process, the House is the grand jury, and the Senate conducts the trial. They must approve foreign treaties negotiated by the president and approve all federal appointees by the executive branch. The Senate cannot originate revenue-based bills.

The Senate is like a pride of lions in the Serengeti. The male lions spend much of their waking hours patrolling and marking their territory by rubbing against trees to attach their scent or spraying urine. They also spend time sniffing for the smell of an intruder or roaring to get the attention of other lion prides to warn them of getting too close. They spend the rest of their time forcing other members of the pride away from the kill and gorging themselves. That certainly describes a significant number of entrenched U.S. Senators.

.

We must amend the Constitution to put term limits in place for Senators, with a maximum of two 6-year terms. Congress is not going to impose an amendment to the Constitution for term limits on themselves unless we replace them with a new generation of congressmen and women who must be vocal and speak out both publicly and privately about our need for change. That is beginning to happen, to some degree, in the lower house. We should encourage that rhetoric.

Members of the Senate and House of Representatives frequently attach spending bills that will benefit only one small group to laws that have strong overall support. They also attach bills creating tax loopholes for a select group or business sector. Many bills have dozens of attached spending bills, such as "a bridge to nowhere." Many of those spending attachments cost hundreds of millions of dollars. The president needs to have the power to veto a line item. It is only possible through a constitutional amendment, and it must originate in the house and senate.

It is going to be a challenge, but one which I consider essential. Presidents Reagan and Clinton asked Congress for this authority, but it never happened.

Political advertising is pervasive and sickening. It seldom focuses on the real issues and is frequently cynical and abusive. It should be banned. We banned it in the tobacco industry, and we can also ban it in political advertising too, which would also be a cost-effective method of reducing political campaign spending.

Legislators and other government officials frequently become lobbyists when leaving office or retiring. Congress needs to pass a law forbidding those highly paid lobbyist positions.

We must modify how candidates run for office in both the executive and legislative branches. The current process is very cumbersome and expensive. We have entered a new technological age, and we should embrace it to modify and streamline the electoral process. Much of the financing of political campaigns is done by political action committees funded by corporations, labor groups, segments of our industrial and economic system, or other special groups. The super PACs contribute to a candidate, and the lobbyists descend upon Washington to seal the deal. Usually, the bills they support or recommend benefit or protect some, but often are harmful to others. A summary of the proposed changes for the legislative and executive branches are as follows:

- An amendment to the Constitution for term limits of the House to five two-year terms.

- An amendment to the Constitution for term limits of Senate members to two six-year terms.
- A constitutional amendment limiting the president and vice-president to one six-year term.
- Ban political advertising.
- Pass a law banning congresspeople, executives, or other high-level government officials from becoming lobbyists after leaving office or retiring.
- A bill banning lobbyists from Washington D.C. That will be tough to achieve.
- Abolish super PACs and their contributions to candidates or political parties. Individual donations would be the only financial support and limit personal contributions to $2500 per candidate or $5000 to any political party
- Outrageously expensive legislative and presidential campaigns are now the norm. Increasing the number of debates is a good plan followed by a question-and-answer series by some news channels such as NPR or others. Wealthy candidates who finance their campaigns could be problematic. The way to control spending by all candidates, wealthy or otherwise, is passing a bill limiting expenditures on campaigns.
- An amendment to the constitution giving the president line-item veto power.

This addresses many of the issues involving the executive and legislative branches. Change won't be easy or quick, and there will be tremendous blowback from some candidates and political parties. Long term politicians will yell and scream like the turmoil associated with taking food from a hungry puppy. These changes are crucial. We can accomplish this in our democratic system without firing a single shot. To succeed, we need millions of citizens who believe change is essential but support a Democratic government and capitalist economy.

TAXES – PERSONAL, CORPORATE, AND INHERITANCE

No one likes, enjoys, or looks forward to paying taxes. One person points across the street and says, "Tax him, not me." Tax loopholes are another severe problem. You are asking someone else to pick up the slack. Our current federal income tax system is riddled with tax loopholes, irrational and almost incomprehensible legalese, and modifications and amendments almost ad infinitum. Our tax system is not fair or equitable. Our personal federal income tax system has been slowly and systematically bastardized to the point that it is embarrassing. The problem can be solved. We all witness and experience the stress and frustration associated with the filing of a tax return. Much of it is due to knowing that the system is unfair, and many are not paying their share.

The House Ways and Means Committee should appoint a committee whose goal is to rewrite our individual and corporate tax code thoroughly. Membership should be composed of two legislators chosen from the House or Senate, two legal professors whose field of endeavor is tax law, and an additional attorney who specializes in legal tax services and litigation. Other members could be an accountant, economist, and individuals with a history of significant achievement in their field of endeavor. The committee would have the goal of completely overhauling our tax system. Construct a new platform that is simple, straightforward, understandable, and fair. Eliminate all existing tax loopholes. Those companies or business sectors benefiting from the tax loopholes will yell, scream, dump money by the wheelbarrow, and threaten Armageddon. Do not listen to them; their opinion is biased. Lobbyists should not be permitted to contact any members of this committee.

For unmarried individuals, the first $25,000 should be tax-free and then taxed at 25% up to $50,000. From 51,000-$400,000 30% rate, and $401,000 to $500.000 at 40% and $501,000 to $1million 45% and $1 million to $5 million 55 %. Anything over $5 million 60%.

A married couple tax-free amount would be $40,000, and the tax rate the same as single individuals—no deductions for children.

Eliminate the deduction for mortgage interest expense. Long-term investments should be encouraged but add 5% to the long-term capital gains tax rate. Qualified dividends are taxed at both the corporate and individual level. The current rate should remain the same.

An alternative minimum tax is necessary for those whose income is almost entirely from qualified dividends, long-term capital gains, or other passive income, and taxed at a lower rate than earned income. The alternative minimum tax should kick in at $500,000. Billionaire Warren Buffett's income is almost entirely passive. His current tax rate is about 14 or 15%, and he admits this is not fair and should be changed.

The corporation tax should be 30%, and all loopholes closed. Adjustments of current depreciation schedules should be made where appropriate. American corporations that operate in other nations around the globe and do not return their earnings to the United States are problematic. If there is an escape route to avoid higher tax rates, and it's relatively safe and secure, a certain percentage of corporations will take advantage of it. We should close those escape routes. Hillary Clinton proposed a plan that addressed this problem, and perhaps it is worth revisiting. Tax loss carryforwards should also be abolished.

Inheritance tax is a delicate issue and one which we must address. The world needs very few billionaires, and those who are privileged to have accumulated hundreds of millions of dollars should be discouraged from passing it onto future generations. In keeping with that philosophy, I recommend the following:

- The first $5 million of inheritance would be tax-free.
- $5 million-$50 million taxed at 40%.
- Tax any amount above $50 million at 80%.

This would encourage the super-wealthy to create a charitable trust or donate those funds to a charitable organization. Bill Gates and Warren Buffett are doing that voluntarily, and others should be strongly encouraged to do the same.

WEALTH DISTRIBUTION, POVERTY, AND HOMELESSNESS.

Wealth distribution in the US is unequal, unfair, and unjust. The top 1% control 40% of the wealth, and the remaining 99% control 60%, and the condition is becoming worse. This disproportionate distribution of wealth in the United States is probably not going to be tolerated by the new generation. Our Neo-liberal capitalist system has permitted it to happen. You can hear and feel the anger in some of the Democratic presidential candidates, and their recommended solutions sometimes go too far and would have serious consequences.

We absolutely must have a national minimum wage. How can you pay a clerk at a grocery outlet $10 an hour when the poverty level for an American family is $25,700. Because of low wages, we are perpetuating and adding to the poverty problem. The national minimum wage should be $15 per hour and be reevaluated and adjusted every five years. We also need a recommended minimum pay scale for various employment levels and skills. Probably about ten different work levels would be appropriate.

The salary of many CEOs and other high-level corporate executives is outrageous and out of control. A cap, a strong suggestion not a rule or regulation, of ten million with compensation above and beyond that amount from stock options or dividends would be reasonable. Those unwilling to abide by that cap level would not qualify for bidding on government contracts. That may sound harsh, but it is necessary and appropriate.

No person or family needs one billion dollars. Wealth accumulation should not be discouraged, but the super-wealthy should become very scarce. More equitable distribution of wealth among the populace, in general, is vital. There is a significant degree of urgency in these recommendations because many U.S. Citizens are very concerned about our unequal wealth distribution.

There are approximately 38 million American citizens at or below the poverty level. Think about that for a moment, and then enjoy your dry-aged prime medium rare New York Steak tonight. A national minimum wage is a beginning, but not the total solution. Gangs, drugs, and violence are pervasive throughout the poverty zones, and that contributes to the overall problem — recommendations for these issues will be discussed later. Our best hope, for now, is education, job training, and some type of financial support where necessary. If we address this issue now, this current generation may be the last to flounder in the fields of poverty and despair.

Homelessness has become a significant issue in most sections of the country. There are currently 58,000 homeless people in Los Angeles County alone, and driving into the central part of Los Angeles or along the Santa Ana riverbed in Orange County is appalling, disgusting, and embarrassing. The trash, the filth, mental illness, widespread drug use, rodents, are overwhelming. Our leaders speak high rhetoric, but they do nothing but kick the bucket down the road. We must construct some housing for these unfortunate individuals. Each compound must also have a free medical clinic, an addiction rehabilitation center, and a mental health facility. If you don't provide those services, you are never going to solve the problem. The funding for this program must be a combination of local and federal and, hopefully, some private donations.

In 2018 there were over 59,000 children in foster care in California. This is a shocking and challenging issue. If we implement many of the changes and programs recommended, these issues will gradually become less problematic. We have not treated this as a crisis yet, but we must soon. A gradual, slow, and deliberate process is required – not some fly-by-night pie-in-the-sky solution. Our leaders can brag, lie, and deceive us for as long as we let them, and instead of making America first, how about making American citizens first. America can take care of itself, but our homeless and poverty-stricken citizens are in a rut, and currently, no rescue plan is available.

MEDICAL CARE DELIVERY SYSTEM

In 2018 Americans spent $3.65 trillion or $11,262 per person for healthcare. Our healthcare costs have been increasing by at least 10% each year, which is several times the inflation rate. Our system is out of control and unsustainable. Some 2020 presidential candidates recommended free medicare for all, and then proceed to tell us that corporations and the super-wealthy will pay for it. They are mistaken, and they know it. To implement such a radical change is not only unaffordable but would significantly disrupt several segments of our economy. There would be chaos and many unforeseen significant problems. Some major changes are necessary and soon. It is difficult to understand how our elected leaders have let this system deteriorate to its current level, not necessarily quality of care, but affordability and availability.

Every citizen must be required to have medical insurance coverage, no exceptions, and it must be affordable. Here is a typical example of our existing system; a 21-year-old male riding a motorcycle on a freeway is involved in a collision with another vehicle, which results in life-threatening injuries. He is transported to a local community health center and hospitalized for three weeks, one week of which is in the intensive care unit, and he has three major surgical procedures. After two weeks, he is considered transportable, but the local county hospital facility has no beds. The total cost of hospitalization is $250,000, and our patient has no medical insurance. This example is not an isolated incident; it and other similar issues occur many times daily. Who pays for this? You and me. How? In high insurance premiums.

Family insurance coverage must extend to all children who are in full-time educational programs regardless of age.

A single-payer program patterned after Medicare must be available to all citizens, but it would not be free. The premium would be based upon your income with those below the poverty level paying little or nothing, and those in the middle class and above paying based upon the projected actual cost of the insurance. It would be significantly less than our current premiums because the young and mostly healthy would be part of the program. Drug supplement programs would be available but optional. For those enrolled in a single-payer health plan, the employee and employer contributions for senior medicare would continue and be increased from the current 1.45% to 1.75%.

The private insurance programs for individuals and families would remain intact for those who wished to continue with non-single payer programs. I estimate about 40-50% of enrollees would opt for the single-payer system and the remaining stay with private insurance. If all citizens were required to have insurance, including the young and healthy, insurance premiums would drop dramatically.

Emergency room visits are incredibly expensive; the system is overcrowded and over-utilized. With a few simple changes, we could reduce our emergency room utilization by at least 75%. To discourage emergency room visits, several changes are necessary.

Urgent care centers must be everywhere, possibly including major chain pharmacies. Most urgent care centers should have lab facilities, radiology services, an ultrasound device, and in the larger centers, a CT scan machine.

Large numbers of the uninsured go to the emergency room for minor problems to avoid the fees associated with private care. When those individuals are required to have insurance, emergency room visits will drop significantly.

The paramedics on 911 calls should have the option of transporting patients to an emergency room or an urgent care facility, based upon the paramedics' assessment of the medical condition. The patient's wishes could override the paramedic decision unless the medic determines the situation is life-threatening. An emergency room visit might cost $5,000, but that same visit at an urgent care center could cost less than $500.

The services of physician assistants (PA), nurse practitioner (NP), registered nurse first assistant (RNFA), and registered nurse anesthetists (CRNA) should be readily available. They should also be licensed to provide services as an independent practitioner, rather than under the direct supervision of a physician. Reimbursement for those services should be less than those offered by a medical doctor.

Virtual visits should be expedited and encouraged. Fifty percent or more routine doctor visits for minor issues could be virtual. The reimbursement for a virtual visit should be considerably less than a personal visit to the facility — much less human resources and other services necessary. Physician Assistants or Nurse Practitioners could provide most of these services. Reimbursement for physician assistant and nurse practitioner services should be less than a medical doctor.

Many diagnostic procedures, especially blood tests, are outrageously expensive. Except for the drawing of blood, blood testing has become fully automated and digitized. Compared to 40 years previously, the number of employees and the space required is much less, but prices have escalated dramatically. Two companies control the blood testing business, and that represents a monopoly. We need at least three new companies vying for the business, and then prices would drop significantly. Theranos Corporation promised to do just that, but unfortunately, it was a hoax and scam with false advertising claims contrived by dishonest management.

Drug pricing is such an outrageous, and greed infested industry that it is embarrassing and distressing. High drug pricing adversely affects almost everyone. How and why we have let this critical issue happen is troubling and disconcerting. Pharma industry lobbying is the most powerful and well funded in Washington. It is much larger than the Oil Industry or Technology, and they have been very successful. Some significant changes are required. Many relatively short duration cancer treatment programs now cost $150,000 for the drugs alone. Here is another example of the absurdity: pharmaceutical company ABC manufactures a drug called Zelda D. In the United States, it sells for $10 per capsule, but in Canada, you can purchase the same drug made by the same company for $1.50. When questioned, the response is always the same: "We must recoup the cost of our research and development, testing, and FDA approval process." I then ask the question, "Why do you sell it in Canada for $1.50, and I have to pay $10? Are you selling it as a loss leader in Canada?" The room is usually so quiet you could hear a toothpick drop. Let's go straight to the fix.

- Reduce the current drug patent term from 20 to 15 years.
- Human drug testing should be performed only in teaching facilities, and well-established medical clinics such as Mayo Clinic, Harvard Medical Center, UCLA, WD Anderson, and others. Drug testing programs by individual physicians or small medical groups can potentially be problematic. If you pay me enough money to put my oldest son through college, I might be just slightly biased in my reporting. I am not paranoid, but I am a skeptic.
- We must reverse federal legislation prohibiting Medicare from negotiating drug pricing.
- Pharmaceutical companies must be prohibited from purchasing generic drug manufacturers. Pharmaceutical companies buy generic

manufacturers and either close them down or increase the price of the generic drug to almost the equivalent of the patented prescription. Any pharmaceutical company currently owning a generic manufacturer must be required to divest themselves of that company.

Drug pricing is a monster that is controlling our money to a degree I would never have believed possible. These additional proposed regulations would apply to new drugs submitted for approval by the FDA.

The FDA would generate a computer profile of the drug, with a suggested wholesale price range. Massive amounts of data are available in this technological age, and the projection should be relatively accurate. At least 50% of the cost of research for new drugs comes from NIH grants, but pharmaceutical companies never mention this. The negotiation process would begin, and if the pharmaceutical company would not agree to an amount near the FDA figure, that patent would then be placed in the public domain and offered to bid to other pharmaceutical companies, with the lowest FDA approved bidder getting the contract. The original patent holder would receive 15% of the wholesale revenue for the next 15 years. In cases of significant disagreements in pricing, the pharmaceutical company holding the patent could provide data that might contradict that of the FDA. This process would force pharmaceutical companies to set reasonable prices rather than espouse their BS

Drug pricing must be treated as a public utility and require approval from the FDA for any price increases.

These proposed changes would significantly expand the role of the FDA, which could be problematic, but it is necessary considering the magnitude of our drug pricing crisis. The pharmaceutical industry will yell, scream, pound on your door, and lobby you to the extreme, but don't listen to them. It isn't the end of the world; it is just a method of controlling greed.

Importing drugs from other countries would also help to solve the outrageous drug prices in the U.S. Pharmaceutical companies would then be forced to reduce drug prices to compete.

The distribution of drugs is also a monopoly and must be corrected. A monopoly of any kind breeds greed, gluttony, arrogance, and elevated prices, and nothing beneficial to the public.

CRUMBLING INFRASTRUCTURE

The definition of infrastructure includes national freeways, local roadways, utilities, bridges, waterways, and sanitation services. Much of this infrastructure was installed 40 to 50 years previously and is deteriorating, crumbling, and unsafe. The current projected cost of repair over ten years is $10.4 trillion and is a local, state, and national obligation. The price will probably be much more as the process develops. The roads in the city I live in are slowly deteriorating and becoming unsafe. Our nationwide rating of infrastructure is only D+. In California, some funds earmarked for road and infrastructure rebuilding have been hijacked and assigned to other state departments. The Trump administration promised two trillion dollars for infrastructure, but, as usual, nothing has happened. When asked where the $2 trillion was coming from, Trump replied, "We will reduce the budget of other programs." Total nonsense. That will never happen in this administration— typical political rhetoric and prattle. If politicians say something often enough, some people will start to believe it. Infrastructure repair will be a huge hurdle. Our infrastructure deterioration is near a crisis, and we must address it.

Here are approaches to fund the staggering cost of infrastructure rebuilding.

- Increase the federal gasoline tax from its current 18.4 cents per gallon to 30 cents. That will be a temporary fix because, within 5-10 years, most vehicles will be electric. Even if short-lived, this tax increase will help.
- Reduce funding for some government departments. I will discuss this in more detail in another chapter.
- Sell municipal infrastructure repair bonds. This would work for utilities and some bridges and waterways. It would not be appropriate for local roadways and freeways.
- Federal bonds would increase our national debt, already approaching troubling levels. I would support it to a modest degree.
- Add $200 billion in our annual federal budget for infrastructure repair and rebuilding.

A single suggestion concerning infrastructure rebuilding will not solve the problem. None are desirable, but we must confront this crisis and soon.

RETIREMENT PLANS, SOCIAL SECURITY, AND LABOR UNIONS

If some of the previous recommendations caused blowback, this section will be significantly worse. Sixty-five percent of American families have less than $5000 in a retirement savings account. Many of them have nothing. Social Security will be facing bankruptcy by 2037. Increased longevity and an increased number of Americans living in retirement have created the problem. Many municipalities, corporations, and states do not have sufficient funding for their defined benefit and pension plans. It is a complicated and challenging issue that we must address. We are approaching a crisis, and if you look around the corner, you can see it staring you in the face. Each category will be discussed separately.

Social Security is the first issue and the most manageable. We must tackle this now before it becomes a crisis. Politicians will be very reluctant to deal with it. The Social Security Trust Fund will run out of cash in 2020 and necessitate drawdown from their reserve account. The current contribution rate is 6.2% for the employer and employee. Three things will solve the problem.

- Gradually increase payroll tax from its current 6.2% to 8.2% over ten years. Start by increasing it to 6.4% in 2021. The increase would apply to both employer and employee.
- Eliminate the current cap of $127,500 on income. All earned income, regardless of the amount, would be taxed. That would generate significant additional funds.
- Allocate 25% of the funds to the stock market. The compounded annual rate of return of the stock market has averaged 9.5% over the last 30 or 40 years. The annualized return of the Social Security Trust Fund is 2.8%. Long-term stock investments significantly outperform bond holdings.

Labor union issues will be very controversial. In the 19th century and early part of the 20th-century, labor unions were necessary. John D. Rockefeller and many others were abusing our labor force beyond anything reasonable or civil. The labor union movement suffered much turmoil and violence, trying to establish their credibility. It worked, and we should be grateful and proud of their accomplishments. Times change and our needs change, and we must adapt. Many federal and local laws rules and regulations now protect the American worker.

Labor unions should not be permitted to represent federal, state, or municipal employees.

Reverse the requirement that construction or other companies that bid on local or federal contracts must be unionized. The current policy tends to create a monopoly, i.e., the only companies that can bid are large unionized firms.

Pensions and benefit retirement plans were once necessary, and a great solution to a serious problem, just as Medicare was for people over the age of 65 who could not purchase insurance.

Most defined benefit plans and pension plans were implemented because of labor demands during negotiation or strikes. They were once necessary; however, a problem arises when pro-labor politicians get elected and pass laws to expand the benefits beyond affordability. Many municipalities will be faced with insolvency in the next 5-10 years because they are unable to meet their pension obligations. Abuse of these plans is common. For example, a fireman captain is scheduled for retirement the following year. His or her retirement income is based upon a percentage of revenue in the year with the highest income level. His superiors give him many hours of overtime or special assignments, and his salary could be 40% or more than in previous years.

Unions sometimes collaborate with investment advisory firms to get kickbacks from the management fees charged, and this can result in costs as high as 2.5% annually, which is outrageous and almost criminal. It is unfair and unjust to the worker. I would not terminate the programs for current long-term employees (over 15 years), which would be very disruptive. Not all actions by labor unions are for the benefit of workers.

We should continue the benefit plans for specific groups but make some modifications. Those who risk their lives to protect us should remain in the defined benefit system, and that includes the military, police officers, and firefighters. Still, we must make changes to eliminate abuse. The law making most retirement income for law enforcement and the military must be abolished.

Retirement planning, one of our most critical issues, is the final subject of this section. If we implement the following recommendations, millions of American citizens will benefit. The stress, strife, and fear associated with insufficient revenue to support a reasonable lifestyle after retirement is a significant issue. Social Security is a useful and valuable retirement program; however, Social Security benefits are not sufficient for the average American family. This solution will only work if it is mandatory for everyone. Some very talented people have calculated that the average employee or small business owner should place 25% of their gross income in a retirement fund. That may be a startling figure, but it isn't as bad as it sounds. You're already saving 12.4% as a contribution from you and your employer to SSA, and you only need an additional 12.5%.

From the first day of employment, the employee would save 7% in a 401(k), or its equivalent, and the employer would match it with 5%. This program would continue until retirement. The only exception might be those at or below the poverty level. It would be one of the greatest things to ever happen to the American worker, and it does not create an unmanageable burden. It must be mandatory for everyone, or it will not work.

THE MILITARY-INDUSTRIAL COMPLEX

The manufacture and distribution of military equipment is a massive industry. The United States federal budget for 2019 was $4.4 trillion, and the deficit was $1 trillion. The Department of Defense's budget for 2019 is $683 billion. The Russian military budget for 2019 is $21.5 billion. The US military budget is equal to the military expenditure of the next 75 nations combined. We also provide military equipment to several other friendly countries around the globe. In the fiscal year 2017, the United States provided $49 billion in financial and military aid to 20 countries. $3.91 billion went to Israel and equal amounts to Iraq and Afghanistan. The NATO alliance created after World War II still exists, and the United States has 70,000 military personnel in the European field and many additional civilian employees. Total cost $24.4 billion annually: that alone is more than the entire Russian military budget. Think about that while we discuss some other points.

The United States assumed the role of the European protectorate after the German, Japanese, and Italian alliance almost destroyed the European Community in World War II. Our goal was to protect the area from a very aggressive Soviet Communist regime. That probably was necessary then, but is it needed now? Seriously doubt it. Should we be the world's protector? I do not think so. Everything changes with time and boots on the ground are yesterday's war, not today's except for special operations forces and peacekeeping forces. Future wars will be fought from the air, the seas, and possibly even the exosphere. Weapons of war will be missiles, bombs, and lasers delivered by autonomous aircraft (drones), submarines, and a few ocean surface vessels. Our new fighter jets are so outrageously expensive and require so much maintenance that we must reduce the number of fighter aircraft.

Our Naval fleet is mostly obsolete and should be replaced by smaller stealth vessels with missiles and drones on board. We do not need the giant destroyers and battleships that we currently deploy all around the world. Aircraft carriers give you great bragging rights, but they are mostly obsolete and very vulnerable to an enemy such as Russia or China that can launch an avalanche of weapons against the vessel.

In 2017 the US had more than 4000 weapons in their atomic arsenal, and Russia was not far behind. The remaining countries have a combined small fraction of the total of the US and Russia. The US has deployed its atomic weapons all around the globe. The energy in our nuclear weapons is more than needed to destroy every animal and plant species on earth. In addition to our current nuclear arsenal, there are multi-thousands of atomic weapons left over from the '50s, '60s, and '70s that are considered obsolete and scheduled for dismantling, but it never happened. Our political leaders once again failed us, leaving us victims of their negligence.

We should all be concerned and troubled by this situation. We must make some changes. *The fix* will be painful, lengthy, and adversarial, but with strength, determination, and resolve, we can effect change and make a difference. Rather than waving banners, yelling into megaphones, and marching in the streets, encourage some new and younger citizens to run for office, and then vote for them. We must aggressively push for change. Here are the recommendations.

- Reduce our military budget now by 25%, and within 5-10 years, reduce that to 50% of the current expenditure. We must acknowledge that warfare has changed.
- Slowly reduce the NATO alliance and within five years have it at about 25% of the current cost.
- Reduce our financial support for countries currently on our subsidy list, and over five years, end the funding.
- Dismantle significant numbers of our current military aircraft and other military equipment. Many are obsolete, and large numbers are not needed.
- Retire many of our unnecessary and obsolete naval vessels and replace them with smaller stealth vessels. Currently, Russia has one operational aircraft carrier, and China also has only one. The United States has 11 nuclear-powered carriers, each carrying 80 fighter aircraft. How can we possibly need that many aircraft carriers in this modern age? It is absurd.

- Discard the idea that we are the world's protector – we do not need to be, and we cannot afford to be. Communism is not sustainable long-term. Currently, there are only five nations worldwide who are communist, and within ten years, it will probably be down to two, or perhaps even one.
- Our military-industrial complex is a monster, and, as is true of most monsters, they are incredibly territorial. It must be slowly downsized. The only way that will happen is to elect a president who believes in downsizing and modernizing the military and will appoint a director of the Department of Defense who thinks along similar lines. Military officers and war machine manufacturers will yell, scream, shout, and lobby. Don't pay any attention to them.
- Dismantle part of our atomic arsenal, even if it's unilateral. Begin with the obsolete nuclear weapons and then slowly proceed to our current stockpile.

PRISON SYSTEM

There are 2.3 million incarcerated individuals in our federal and state prisons, juvenile detention centers, and local jails. The system is overcrowded, underfunded, often antiquated, and unworkable. Approximately 300,000 are for drug addiction or drug-related offenses. Many prisons are overcrowded, and each year thousands of inmates are released early due to overcrowding.

My focus is on those incarcerated for drug addiction and drug-related offenses. Drug addiction should not be a criminal offense unless violence against others is involved. The average annual cost of incarceration of a prisoner in the United States is $31,000. If you multiply $31,000 times 300,000, the total is $9.3 billion. Drug addiction is a massive problem in the United States. It has been for several decades but recently received much public awareness due to the manufacture and sale of vast amounts of opioids. In the past, drug addiction was more common on the East Coast and West Coast, but the opioid addiction problem involves large areas of middle America and smaller towns in the eastern US. A pharmacy in a small town in Iowa recently dispensed enough opioids in one year to provide several hundred tablets for every resident.

Except for alcohol and tobacco, we have labeled most drug addiction as a criminal offense. In addition to violent crime (gangs and drug cartels), there are multi-thousands of so-called petty thefts committed each year to obtain money to purchase addictive substances. Mental health issues such as anger control, paranoia, schizophrenia, and bipolar disorder are also frequent components of drug addiction. You will never control drug addiction by passing a law making it a criminal offense or incarcerating the offenders.

Drug addiction is a medical problem, not a felony or a misdemeanor. Due to prison overcrowding, thousands of drug offenders are being released back into the public arena each year. Early release is appropriate, but releasing them directly into their last environment leads to a resumption of their former lifestyle, usually involving drugs and often crime and theft. If you talk with a substance abuse addict who has been sober for several years, and you ask him or her, "How often do you think of drugs during the day?" The answer will be, "Dozens of times, and sometimes continuously." Until we accept the fact that substance abuse and drug addiction are a medical and mental health issue, we will never control it. My recommendations follow.

- Build more mental health facilities across the nation.
- Construct multiple safehouses or temporary housing facilities for those drug-dependent inmates released from prison, or individuals required to have drug treatment programs mandated by judges.
- Provide ongoing medical treatment and education programs beginning before their release.

- Those released early would be required to remain in a safe house for at least six months. During that time, provide free drug or alcohol rehabilitation services and mental health counseling and treatment.
- Previous inmates would also be required to participate in supervised online education or job training programs.
- Provide financial aid to all parolees for twelve months. They would also be permitted unsupervised excursions to visit family, friends, or purchase personal items. GPS ankle devices would be mandatory for unsupervised outings.
- Perform frequent random drug testing. Two positive tests would be a violation of parole.
-

Will all these changes happen soon? Highly unlikely, but it could be a platform for the future. Unless we elect a new generation of legislators and leaders, probably most of these changes will not happen. If we do not make some changes soon, a real crisis will occur, and that crisis is already on our doorstep with its hand on the doorknob. Drug addiction is a global problem. It's a war, whether you like it or not, and regardless of what President Obregon of Mexico says, we are not going to win this war with the drug cartels by peace, love, and understanding. We all know how well that is going! Most poppy growers and cocaine distributors are not peace-loving people but are drug warlords, whose lives are teeming with murder, violence, bribery, and corruption. Eradicating the growers and distributors of opioids and other addictive substances will require a worldwide effort. It is difficult to conceal the growing fields and processing plants, but it is easy to hide the finished product distributed in small batches.

IMMIGRATION AND UNDOCUMENTED
IMMIGRANTS

There are 11.1 million undocumented immigrants in the United States. President Trump has tweeted and said many times, "There are some bad people among our illegals." He speaks the partial truth, but the overwhelming majority are decent, productive, law-abiding people.

Of those millions of undocumented immigrants, many live in fear and anxiety concerning themselves and their families. I know several families who have children, some undocumented, and others are citizens because they were born here. They represent a significant and essential workforce. President Trump says, "Go home, apply for legal immigration, and wait your turn." That return time is now at a near standstill, and the chances of their returning legally are slim to none. Trump's attitude wreaks of paranoia; he says they come here to harm us, and let's lock them up and throw away the key. The last time we successfully dealt with this problem was 1986 when we granted amnesty to 3.8 million undocumented immigrants, which led to eventual citizenship for most.

There are several ways to rectify our undocumented immigrant problem. I am not a proponent of illegal immigration, but since we have permitted it and continue to do so, we must deal with the problem. Prosecuting, and deporting 11 million people is an impossible task unless you take a page from Adolf Hitler's playbook, and put them in concentration camps. However, granting amnesty and subsequently creating a pathway to citizenship is a workable solution. We are a nation of immigrants, and that's what makes us great. My wife and I occasionally attend school programs involving our grandchildren, and you see multiple children from different ethnic backgrounds, being treated equally, and performing together. It is indeed a memorable and enjoyable experience. I believe amnesty and then opening the road to citizenship is the only rational and reasonable approach.

Require all undocumented immigrants to apply for amnesty, and those who do not apply or are gang members are the bad guys who will be deported. The applicants would be granted amnesty and guided toward the path of citizenship. Whether they have paid taxes is not essential. The past is the past, and if they are law-abiding and decent people, we should welcome them to the United States.

After granting amnesty, we must make a serious effort to close our borders. Mr. Trump wants to build a $10 billion wall, and that may help temporarily, but all walls eventually crumble either naturally or with assistance. If we deploy drones with heat-seeking and other advanced technological devices, I think we could mostly solve the problem. So long as we remain a nation of opportunity, freedom, social and economic justice, others will seek us out, and some will be so desperate they cross our borders illegally. It seems unreasonable for a person who needs to or wants to immigrate should wait 10-15 years.

NATIONAL BASIC INCOME

Some Nations have discussed basic income for several years. One American Democratic presidential candidate is proposing a national basic income of $1000 per month for all adult American citizens. The annual cost would be $396 billion. I have studied and researched national basic income for the past two years, and the data from one South African country is impressive. Namibia previously instituted a basic income program of US $40 per month, and a German Church organization funded it.

The statistics are fascinating – many more children attended school, far fewer were malnourished, and the crime rate dropped by 42%. In the United States, the citizens of Alaska have been receiving annual stipends from oilwell revenue since 1984. The amounts are not enough to be considered basic income, more like a subsidy.

National basic income is a scientifically untested method of eradicating poverty. We could and should introduce it on a limited scale, such as five million adults below the poverty level. We could do this without significant stress on our national debt. Anyone with a history of alcohol or drug addiction would be required to attend a weekly alcohol or drug addiction free clinic. Random drug testing would be performed and would drop repeat positive testing offenders from the program. This may seem cruel but is unwise to subsidize long term alcohol or drug abuse. All enrollees currently unemployed would be enrolled in a free online educational and job training program, monitored by social services. Social services should be intimately involved in implementing the plan and collecting data. We could probably rescue 50% or more of those below the poverty level and realize significant benefits from the program. If some of the other recommendations, especially national minimum income, are implemented, that will also have a substantial impact on poverty levels.

I find it almost inconceivable that the wealthiest nation on earth has 38 million adults and children below the poverty level.

STUDENT LOAN DEBT

The student loan debt in the United States is $1.4 trillion. Most debtors are young people in college, graduate school, or recent graduates who have never been or just recently employed. Can you imagine beginning your adult life with $100,000 in debt hovering over your head? The fear and terror that so many of our young people experience is dreadful.

Congress initiated the student loan program in 1965, and the goal was admirable, and the concept appropriate for the time, but, as usual, our politicians expanded it. There are now multiple types of student loan programs, including Federal, Perkins, private lenders, and other smaller ones. There are also some family student loan programs where the parents have the burden for repayment. As so often happens with government programs, nonprofit and for-profit higher education teaching facilities saw this program as a windfall. They seized the opportunity to raise their tuition and fees dramatically. Repayment is usually delayed until graduation or until the recipient has been a student less than 50% of the time. Some have a grace period of several months after graduation. In some, the interest is compound, which means interest is added to the principal, and recipients pay interest on the interest, which can be devastating over a several year timespans.

It is almost impossible to discharge student loans with bankruptcy, and the only way to avoid repayment is to leave the country, which some students are doing. The delinquency rate is significant. Our current situation is intolerable and absolutely must be corrected. It is a horrible burden on many brought about by an expanded program initially aimed at solving a specific problem. Here are the recommendations:

- Abolish the current plan and replace it with federal grants. Visibility requirements should be quite strict; otherwise, it will be abused.
- The federal government would liquidate the current loans over ten years, but the debtor would be responsible for the interest.
- There are some programs for loan forgiveness, but they are extremely limited and should be expanded.
- States are required to provide free education up through and including high school. We must expand that to include college for state residents who meet the qualifications for higher education.
- Available grants, not federal, must be encouraged from private donors – they will step up to the plate to avoid the 80% tax rate on inheritance. Michael Bloomberg has donated $1.8 billion to Johns Hopkins University. Those funds will be available to dramatically increase

the number of grants available to students who qualify and need them.

 If we implement the above suggestions, the problem will be gradually solved. If we don't do something, this problem will expand, and we will have almost an entire generation of young citizens starting their life journey with massive debt hanging over their heads. We cannot permit that to happen. Complete and immediate loan forgiveness is probably not a viable option; the cost would be high and add to our already substantial budget deficit.

A group of my friends (most all college graduates) were recently at a social gathering discussing the student loan program. Mr. Hensley has three children and all attended college. His youngest just finished college last year, and he said the total cost was $700,000. That is a staggering amount of money, but fortunately, he could afford it, and there is no student debt.

DISCUSSION OF EVERYTHING ELSE

If some changes do not happen, our nation's future is unclear; however, if we make changes quickly guided by emotion and anger, our future is very clear – America has a dismal outlook. Some nations have found a way to have a progressive social system for their citizens, and yet maintain a balanced budget. Still, they do have high personal income tax rates and no significant military expenditure. Our democratic and capitalist system, because of its economic and political advantage, can accomplish the same without unduly punishing the wealthy or completely dismantling our military. A socialist system looks and feels good in the beginning but soon ends in a disaster, usually resulting in massive inflation

We are on the threshold of greatness, but if we use our scientific and technological advances in an unsafe manner (atomic weapons), we may face extinction. Our planet has a long history of dramatic evolutionary expansion of flora and fauna, followed by massive extinctions. We must reach for the former and avoid the latter. Climate change, species extinction, pollution of our environment with waste and toxic chemicals, and we must focus on other issues.

By implementing change and innovation-- along with with a more equitable distribution of wealth, and greatly expanded education-- we will accomplish something exceptional. The grossly unequal distribution of consumable protein is another example – 20% of the world population consumes 80% of the protein.

Our voting system is antiquated and has not kept up with new technological advances. Voting by mail in some states is a start, but it needs expanding and modernization. Registering and voting on the internet or by mail is the answer. Many will say it is unsafe and cannot be controlled or monitored. They are wrong. If I can safely manage my bank account on the internet or purchase a home by using DocuSign, I can also safely vote on the internet. If we could vote on the internet or by mail, many more young people would vote.

Unequal wealth distribution in the US is a complex social, economic, and moral issue. Is it unfair, unjust, and immoral for 1% of the population to control 40% of the wealth? Becoming super-wealthy should not be treated as a criminal offense, but as an unintended consequence of our economic system. The change should be gradual, fair, equitable, and as nonthreatening as possible. If we severely punish the wealthy, we might stifle innovation and progress, and that would be a huge mistake. To revamp the tax code and make it difficult to pass along massive amounts of wealth to future generations, and almost impossible for profitable corporations and the wealthy to avoid taxation will change the attitude and behavior of many of the other 99% of American citizens.

The change should be gradual, fair, equitable, and as non-threatening as possible.

 In a recent CBS 60 Minutes interview with Jamie Dimon, the CEO of J.P. Morgan Chase, he disclosed he had an annual salary of $31 million. He handled the interview quite well, but when confronted, he stated, "I don't make my compensation decision, the Board of Directors does." When asked why he didn't just return some of it, he said, "I don't think that would make a difference." He is correct in both issues, but he probably has more control over the BOD than he disclosed. If we place a rational and reasonable cap on Executive compensation, the psychological impact will be significant. Profitable corporations should also be encouraged to give their employees a bonus occasionally, not in cash, but corporate stock. I think you would see a dramatic change in employee attitude and productivity. Chobani Greek Yogurt Company recently announced a bonus plan.

There are only a few socialist, communist, monarchies, or dynasties around the planet. Socialism works quite well for a few years or even a few decades but will eventually collapse because the citizens vote so many perks and subsidies for themselves that it becomes economically unsustainable. Democracy and capitalism are, by far, the best and the most equitable. Some American-based international corporations have devised a way to avoid most all taxation of profits. Apple is probably the biggest offender, and they did it by establishing a subsidiary in Ireland where the corporate tax rate is only 12.5%, but that isn't the end of the story. They created a mythical cloud-based company in which the Irish subsidiary passed on 95% of the profits to the cloud-based company, and it was nontaxable because it had no physical address. This imaginary entity did have a Board of Directors, and they probably had their meetings in a supersonic aircraft flying at 70,000 feet altitude!! The profits were not returned to the United States, and the products were made and assembled in China, sold around the world, and the profits placed in the cloud but, of course, reported in their annual financial statement. For the world (in this case, the European Union) to permit such shenanigans is shameful, embarrassing, and outrageous. This scheme represents a con with no borders – endless space. Numerous other US-based international corporations have opened subsidiaries in low corporate tax rate countries and avoided the higher US tax rate. It is not a tax loophole; it is a canyon of cash, filled with free money by greedy and devious companies. It is disgraceful. Hillary Clinton did propose a *fix* during the Clinton Presidency, and we might wish to readdress her proposal.

. Lenin- Marxist communism has been around for almost 70 years and is currently practiced (mandated) in only five countries, including China, Vietnam, Cuba, and Russia. North Korea has a communist government, but its leadership is a Dynasty and has been since 1948. We tried to dismantle it in the Korean War, but as so often has happened in recent wars waged by America, the outcome was less than satisfactory. Many communist nations disappeared with the collapse of the Soviet Union; the reason was the Soviet Union was subsidizing the governments, and without that subsidy, they collapsed. Communism will eventually disappear because the slaves (citizens) will ultimately revolt. It happened in Taiwan, and it is happening in Hong Kong at this moment, and Macau could be next. We attempted to eradicate it in Vietnam, but that was also a failure. Monarchies such as Saudi Arabia and Oman are still around, but if you research the history of monarchies, you will find most have disappeared. This trend will continue, and soon, they will all be in the history books – good riddance.

Democracy and capitalism are the future until someone comes up with a better system. If you give an informed citizenry the proper template (Constitution and Bill of Rights) and the freedoms that go with it, they will make the right choices. However, there will be some missteps along the way. We are still working on our democratic system, and there are still a few kinks, but we can gradually correct them. Once someone has experienced democracy, freedom, and a free economy, they never want to go back unless it is to create change in the system of another nation. How many undocumented immigrants do you know that wish to return to their previous land of residence? Probably none.

Democracy and capitalist economic systems are one in which countries trade and share commerce and industry. The currency is mostly controlled by private individuals and businesses rather than the state. It must always encompass property rights, freedom of choice and movement, and encourage change, innovation, and progress. If you combine all of this and impose some rules and regulations that make it work efficiently for everyone, not just a few, you have a winning combination. We mostly have that in America, and it indeed has been a winner. We have the largest economy in the world; our leaders are the most influential and respected, and our citizens are renowned and envied all over the planet.

However, residing at the top of the mountain will not continue unless we make some alterations and changes in our political and economic systems. The American Empire is not yet crumbling, but it has a few significant fractures. Our political and economic system is currently the envy of the world, and that will continue for several centuries, but only if we make some modifications.

Education is the next topic, and it is so important that I could write another book about it. In the dark ages, learning and acquisition of knowledge were severely restricted, and almost the only people who could read and write were landowners, aristocrats, and church leaders. Why would you want to educate a slave, a member of the working class, a king's servant, or members of a large international church where everyone is uneducated, submissive, and listens and obeys every time you speak. If you educate them, their brain becomes energized, curious, and they begin to realize something is not right, and it must be corrected. You then have a revolt on your hands, and the fearless and all-controlling and powerful rulers and leaders become a target. You begin to question their edicts, their dogma, and their supposed infallibility. I doubt the American slaveowners sent any of their South African slaves to school – what slave owner would want to have a slave who could read, write, and think?

We currently have large numbers of children throughout the world who are either undereducated or uneducated, and it is a tragedy of massive proportion and must be corrected. There probably are dozens and perhaps hundreds of geniuses who were previously enslaved or illiterate and never had a chance to benefit the world by their ideas, innovations, and theories. I know two people who are incredibly brilliant but were never encouraged to pursue an education beyond high school and were not able to advance significantly. Some people are so talented and gifted that they don't need much higher education, but they are very few and far between. Education is the key to everything, and I don't mean a communist system where it is more of a training academy. Just teach me physics, don't tell me I will never be a good physicist unless I am also a communist.

We have an incredible, unbelievable, and an almost inexhaustible amount of knowledge available to us 24/7×365. We must disseminate that information. One of the best days of my life would be when every child in the world over the age of 10 could read and write. In earlier times in a polytheistic world, there was a God of almost everything. Then Isaac Newton theorized gravity and the Gods who controlled the sun and the planets gradually disappeared into a chasm of darkness never to be heard from again. Galileo theorized that Earth was not the center of the universe and that it revolved around the sun, not vice versa. The church challenged him and persecuted him, and the only way he saved his life was by stating, "I do not believe what I wrote." Education, original thought, and curiosity are the future, not dogma, all-knowing rulers, or doctrine.

With advanced education and knowledge, our future could be a shining light, but the American educational system is severely lacking in affordable college education. For those deserving students who come from poverty or lower-middle-class families, a tuition free college education is not available unless you qualify for a grant or you take on the responsibility of the student loan debt. That must change-- every state must provide tuition free college education for their student citizens. We mandated it with elementary and high school, and I'm sure we can accomplish the same with higher education. Please support, encourage, and demand education for all. If we don't achieve it, future generations 5000 years from now will depict us as much less progressive and enlightened than we are. Be a part of the future and demand education for everyone everywhere. A knowledgeable, curious, informed, involved, and open-minded populace must be our future.

Now let's move on to another topic. Monopolies, massive corporations, and banks too big to fail with their associated greed are not necessarily interested in the welfare of their customers or clients. They are a breeding ground for power, money, and a desire to control everything. Unfortunately, we have let this happen in the United States. Banks and international corporations that are too big to fail have become commonplace. It is dangerous. Greed associated with unrestrained lending practices and the purchase and sale of derivatives almost upended the American economy in 2008-2009. Packaged mortgages were sold to the public as secure investments when lenders knew borrowers could not possibly repay the loans. When large amounts of money roll in on a wave of greed, it can become a tsunami. A prolonged, very low or negative interest bank rate is also dangerous. Individuals and companies borrow cheap money to expand their business or enter new ventures, which may be risky and unwarranted. It can create an artificial demand which extends beyond our ability to satisfy, and uncontrolled inflation sometimes occurs. I am not opposed to low interest rates – just those that seem unreasonably and unnecessarily low.

A money center bank may look like a regional bank; however, their focus is on large corporations, mergers and acquisitions, other banks, currency, and commodity trading. They have minimal interest in individual borrowers. In a merger and acquisition, involving several billion dollars, two or three major banks will collaborate, and jointly fund the acquisition. Money center banks should not be permitted to own or control brokerage and money management firms or expand by buying local banks. A few money center banks control the money flow over most of the world. J.P. Morgan Chase handles $6 trillion daily, which is more than the annual budget of the 30 smallest countries in the world. One too-big-to-fail bank has 22,500 branches, with 58,000 ATMs.

Six companies virtually control our food industry. They manage and control the price of most food items you purchase. Some of these massive conglomerates have bought and now own 20 or 30 large food companies. We must make some changes in our governmental agencies supervising acquisitions and mergers. We have permitted huge corporations to acquire their competitors on a level not seen in many years, and as a result, many giant international behemoths now control almost everything. Monopoly or near monopoly is very bad for consumers, and too-big-to-fail corporations have become a threat to our economy – remember 2008 and 2009 and the near disaster that occurred. If large corporations stifle competitors, prices tend to stabilize at levels significantly above those of a genuinely competitive market. If one company raises the price on an item, others often follow.

AIG Insurance was a large international insurance group that traded risky credit default swaps, which guaranteed mortgages created by money center and regional banks. Many of these mortgages failed during the 2008-2009 global financial crisis. This failure would have ricocheted throughout many world economies, and we rescued AIG. The Federal Reserve loaned AIG Insurance $85 billion to prevent a catastrophic world economic disaster. Requiring these companies to divest themselves of multiple companies will be disruptive and problematic. However, it must happen, and future acquisitions must be severely restricted. A giant is seldom gentle in its treatment of much smaller rivals. An example, there is a new bakery in town, and customers are raving about their various bread products. The owner wishes to expand his business by placing the bread on the shelves of local supermarkets. It can't happen because the big bread companies have purchased all the shelf space, and the only way he can expand his business is to be acquired by one of the major food suppliers.

Companies such as Amazon, Google, Facebook, Microsoft, and Apple are usually not gentle giants. Once they control almost everything, they can set the price on nearly anything. If Amazon wishes to crush a startup competitor, they will temporarily sell those same products at a loss to put the new company out of business.

Microsoft and Apple control most computer operating software. We need a public domain alternative, and in some cases, we do, however much of the patented software doesn't support it. I subscribe to Microsoft Office 365, and it's a great program, but I probably use less than 20% of its capabilities. An annual fee of $100 for Microsoft Office 365 is not a problem for many Americans; however, in many nations around the globe, it's unaffordable for the average citizen. There are free alternatives such as Libre Office and Google Docs; however, the Nuance voice dictation system I use does not support them, so I'm stuck with Microsoft. I want a public domain software alternative available for those less fortunate than I am. If a viable public domain software were available, Microsoft and Apple would lower their prices. How can we create this public domain software? I am confident that talented retired programmers would donate some of their time to such an endeavor. Elon Musk has placed some of his electric car patents in the public domain – that is a good beginning. I want viable options for those who are less fortunate than myself.

Governmental subsidy programs always get my attention because most of them are unnecessary and benefit only a political group or industry. Once put into place, they are often expanded and continued indefinitely. The farm subsidy program was necessary when instituted many years previously. However, our agricultural industry has changed dramatically. Previously the grain, corn, bean, and cotton industries were very labor-intensive, but now with automated farm planting and harvesting machines, two or three people can cultivate 3,000- 4,000 acres of soybeans. Also, large farming companies now own most small family farms, or agricultural giants manage them.

Government subsidy programs include some surprising names such as Alcoa, Shell Oil Company, Ford Motor Company, Fiat Chrysler, Intel, and Nike. The list is lengthy, and it is difficult to convince me that most are necessary. By eliminating these programs, the government could reduce its annual budget by $100 billion, but it will never happen unless we elect a new generation of government legislators and executives. It is easy to become addicted to a subsidy, and the withdrawal cries will be loud, and lobbyist money will be flowing like an open faucet, but we can accomplish this.

In 1998 there was a $245 billion settlement with the five major tobacco companies. Virtually all funds went to 48 states, District of Columbia, and five territories, and was to be paid over 25 years. Some states became dependent upon this free money to enhance their budgets. These funds were for promoting public awareness of the dangers of tobacco but, guess what; they were hijacked and used by the states for other programs. Two of the tobacco companies threatened to default on payments because their profits and business suffered greatly. Some states, when faced with possible loss of free money, completely changed their attitude and wanted to know what they could do to assist in fixing the problem. Subsidies and free money changes attitudes and sometimes control decision-making.

When Abraham Lincoln declared war against the southern slave states, he did it for the benefit of everyone, not himself, not the Washington politicians, not the Northern Section, but the nation in general. Abraham Lincoln was a Republican. Where have Republicans like him gone? Are they in hiding? Do they not exist? They do exist, and we must find them and encourage them to run for elected office. Only then will change happen.

Another problem our country faces is corruption, bribery, and kickbacks. They are much more common than most people believe, but are mostly hidden and never discovered. We like to think of corrupt practices occurring primarily in Mexico, South American countries, and underdeveloped nations, but it frequently happens in the U.S. and other developed nations. Vladamir Putin has never owned a business and has always been in the communist government hierarchy, but he is one of the wealthiest men on the planet. Another example involves the city of Los Angeles and the homeless problem. Many in the homeless population were depositing fecal material and urine on the sidewalks of downtown LA. To help solve this problem, the city ordered some portable toilets and each station cost between $325,000 and $395,000. You can buy a charming single-family residence in Nashville, Tennessee, for considerably less than $325,000. It is impossible to convince me there was no corruption, collusion, or bribery in that contract. We do incarcerate an occasional politician, but the process remains pervasive.

Several years ago, I was on a fishing trip in an area north of Cabo San Lucas in Baja California Sur, Mexico, and was having my single-engine Cessna aircraft refueled in preparation for departure. Five or six passengers (all men) disembarked from a twin-engine private plane, and while the attendant was refueling that aircraft, I asked the pilot about the passengers. He told me they were members of the city planning department in a city in north central California, and they were here on a fishing trip. I then asked him who hired him, and he said a construction company. Bingo!! There is a partial solution on the horizon, and it involves artificial intelligence. As we become more dependent upon computerized technology, especially artificial intelligence, and less personal decision-making is required, the pervasive corruption and bribery system should slowly get better. I'm not aware of any way you can bribe a robot. There is some hope.

Money and funding are always an issue. Money does matter. Some of the programs recommended require significant capital, and since we already have an enormous budget deficit, how are we going to afford them? Revising the tax code, eliminating tax loopholes, and increasing taxes on the wealthy plus a mild increase in corporate taxes will produce significant revenue. If you add that to the money saved by reducing the military budget and deleting subsidies, there should be no additional deficit even if we implement these changes.

The next few sections involve problems and suggested changes that deal with longer-term issues, some involving not just the United States but the entire world. The United States cannot solve many of these problems alone; it will require global participation and cooperation. President Donald Trump has either canceled or declined to attend some of the conferences involving these issues, but that too, like everything else, will change.

Climate change is the next issue I will discuss. If you ask President Trump about this problem, his answer would probably be, "It's a hoax, don't believe it. Just go about business as usual, and everything will be fine." That may be mostly true for my generation, but not our children and grandchildren. Climate change is real-- the global temperature is slowly rising, atmospheric carbon dioxide levels are dangerously high, the oceans are becoming warmer and more acidic. Water levels are also rising. Natural disasters, including fires, drought, flooding, and hurricanes, are now more frequent and destructive. If we do not develop some device that will convert our atmospheric carbon dioxide excesses into less toxic material, we and our children and their children will have many disrupting and troubling issues. Within 20-30 years, many homes and other structures along the waterfronts of the West Coast and East Coast will be abandoned and crumbling. The same is true for many islands and island nations.

The world populations will move north or south from the equator toward the northern or southern hemispheres, and Greenland could become a thriving metropolitan area. Many areas will be devastated by hurricanes, floods, drought, and rising temperatures. The more acidic ocean waters (absorbed carbon dioxide converted into carbolic acid), will result in massive coral death and the extinction of thousands of ocean species, both animal and plant. It won't be as severe as the Permian extinction, but it will be worldwide and devastating.

Homo sapiens has not yet accepted the obvious global change in climate and made appropriate adjustments before the crisis happens. Florida could become mostly swampland and the island of Nantucket, a flooded wasteland. Humans survived the Ice Age, and we can endure a warming cycle, but the consequences will be long-lasting, devastating, and horrible. Recently, in mid-November, in Southern California, we experienced strong easterly winds, a temperature of 97°, and humidity of 6% along with raging fires throughout much of the state. The East Coast, the northern Midwest, and parts of the South are experiencing record low temperatures for this time of the year. Donald Trump will say, "See I told you, it's a hoax, just look at the people freezing on the East Coast." What he doesn't understand is that climate change involves extremes in both hot and cold, but the overall trend is what's important, and that points to global warming.

Future generations will experience the disruption and devastation caused by climate change, and it could continue for several centuries. The United States has made some progress, but it is inadequate. Many other nations, especially China and Indonesia, continue to produce massive amounts of carbon dioxide and other toxins that aggravate climate change. It is a global problem and requires global awareness and commitment to reducing CO2 emissions.

Our world population is in an explosive phase. Humans living on planet Earth currently number seven billion seven hundred million. It took 200,000 years for the population to reach one billion, and only 200 years more to reach seven billion. It could reach 11 billion by the year 2100. Our current population growth is not sustainable unless something dramatic occurs, such as happened with the agricultural revolution. Many experts agree that the sustainable world population is 4.5 billion. Nature sometimes has a way of correcting extremes. A worldwide influenza outbreak like the one in 1918 would probably kill two billion people today with an infected individual encountering thousands of people while traveling from one continent to the next. Another possibility is a worldwide resistant bacterial infection, but that would be slower and less devastating because it requires direct contact with bodily fluids or excrement.
In contrast, a global flu epidemic is spread by indirect contact such as breathing infected air. Another possibility would be an atomic conflict, or possibly a combination of all three.

We are also on the threshold of outgrowing our food supply unless something dramatic changes. One possibility, and it would change everything, is growing our protein from stem cells. Instead of killing a turkey, you would create a turkey breast from stem cells and then cook it in the oven or crockpot. That would dramatically alter everything, all for the better. There is a significant possibility nature will correct our overpopulation problem, but if not, we must soon address the issue.

Pollution of the planet by toxic chemicals, herbicides, insecticides, sewage, garbage, and plastic are troubling and scary. Significant amounts of toxic chemicals, untreated sewage, trash, and plastic are polluting, littering, and poisoning our planet. In 2018, twenty-two billion discarded single-use plastic water bottles ended up in landfills, incinerators, or the ocean, and if nothing changes by 2100, that number probably will be 33 billion. Who would ever have believed that in the year 2018, one of our most significant concerns would be single-use plastic? Coca-Cola or beer cans, maybe, but water bottles!!

The City Council of Los Angeles is considering banning single-use plastic water bottles, and which would be a great beginning. Single-use plastic is possibly the most significant current threat to our well-being and our future. Plastic takes 1000 years to biodegrade in our landfills or oceans. If we don't modify or ban single-use plastic within 100 years or less, we will be inhabitants of a plastic world. The answer is the development of biodegradable plastic, and I know it's doable. Why are we waiting? There are only two other options, one is to ban it, and the other is to transport and dump it on the moon.

We must tackle these problems now, but, as usual, we probably won't until the situation has become critical. The crisis is now, but we are mostly ignoring it. We pollute many of our waterways and ocean waters along shorelines with toxic chemicals, human waste, and discharged industrial waste, and, as usual, we are not dealing with it on a timely basis. There has been some progress, but it's slow, and there is tremendous resistance from industry, politicians, and insufficient funding.

We also have a huge amount of atomic waste stockpiled around the country, just waiting for some governmental agency, to give a green light for long-term safe storage. Why are we postponing this? We can spend $2.4 trillion on the Iraqi and Afghanistan wars, but we can't properly dispose of our waste products.

If I could tell my long-deceased grandmother the problem, and if she could, she would say, "Get out of here, Jack, you idiot, what's wrong with you? Don't bother me with such garbage (that's a pun)."

Species extinction is another problem which we should and must confront. If you are a paleoclimatologist and you examine the Cliffs of Dover along the English coast, you will see 70 million years of layered chalk, which at one time represented the sediment of the ocean floor. Not surprisingly, you will also see many layers of fossilized ocean creatures. On close inspection, you will notice that the species appears, it's numbers rapidly increase, their overall size increases, and then it disappears to be replaced by another species. This represents species extinction, and it occurs repeatedly. We are not sure, but almost certainly, they outgrew their food supply. Are humans faced with the same potential problem? Possibly yes.

We are causing the extinction of many species. I become nauseated when I see a video of humans starting a fire in the Amazon jungle to clear the land for human habitation, or the growth of corn, or other food for human or animal consumption. We are destroying the wild animal habitat throughout the world by deforestation, species displacement for human habitat, toxic chemicals, the killing of wild animals for pleasure, overfishing our oceans, and blocking herd migration.

We are currently in the Meghalayan age, but many scientists want to rename it an extinction age. We have made some progress in species protection in the last 40 to 50 years, but it is infinitesimal compared to the problem, and most of the world is turning a blind eye rather than confronting the crisis. Destroying a threatened species which has taken millions of years to evolve should be a crime. Many of the lions in the Serengeti and the Kalahari Desert are an endangered species, but when the pride wanders from their protected area in search of food, they are killed for pleasure and bragging rights. Our assistance is needed to help protect our endangered species. Donald Trump and many others will say, "It's our planet, we are the boss of everything, and leave us alone." Do not believe them; they are lying and trying to deceive you. We are the most dominant species that have ever inhabited planet Earth, but we have an obligation and duty to protect it and preserve it for future generations. We should not be gluttons just because we can. We must control our whims and desires and be a productive and aware inhabitant of our planet.

The use of antibiotics on healthy animals is becoming a serious and critical problem, due to the development of antibiotic-resistant bacteria, which can be lethal to humans. The World Health Organization predicts that if we do not alter our current usage of antibiotics that by

2050 the largest killer of humans will be antibiotic-resistant bacteria. Doctors and veterinarians are not the only ones using antibiotics. The companies that produce poultry, pork, and beef for human consumption feed 80% of the antibiotics sold worldwide to their animal population. Many veterinarians also frequently use antibiotics indiscriminately and excessively on your pets, with the possibility of Rover, transmitting antibiotic-resistant salmonella to you and other family members.

In the 1950s, it was determined that feeding antibiotics to animals in sub-therapeutic doses improved the health of animals and accelerated their growth. It resulted in an astonishing increase in the use of antibiotics in healthy animals. In 2007 the World Health Organization began advising countries to reduce antibiotic use in animals produced for food because of the development of antibiotic-resistant bacteria. The European Union has passed a law making it illegal to administer antibiotics to healthy animals that will take effect in 2022. The United States Congress needs to pass a law banning the use of antibiotics in healthy animals grown and produced for human consumption, and at the same time, ban the importation of meat from any country which continues to use antibiotics indiscriminately. It is a critical issue, but again, the change will probably never happen unless we elect some new and younger legislators and executives.

I encourage you to join me in becoming an active middle-of-the-roader and slowly but surely proceed to a better result and life. It could be a beautiful, exhilarating, and rewarding experience. But wait, you haven't quite finished reading yet. I have written a conclusion that is somewhat lengthy and will be challenging, but please consider stepping up to the plate and taking the challenge. You will be, and we all will be deeply rewarded.

CONCLUSION

If you are reading this, you probably have read the book, and that's a start, but it's just the beginning. We must develop and support a plan of action. No massive protests, no screaming into megaphones, no waving of banners is necessary, just millions of us who consistently and relentlessly demand changes to our political and economic system. It does not matter what political party you belong to because this is not a political organization. This is a movement to propose and recommend change, innovation, and modernization. Our method of distribution of information and recommendations should be mostly social media, not the streets, stadiums, or public arenas. Social media can be problematic, but it is the future, and we need to grab the reins and move toward a better, safer, more secure, and fulfilling life. Many of the changes I recommend will not happen unless we elect a new generation of legislators and leaders who concentrate on us, not themselves or their political party. Territorialism, aggressively vying for power and trying to discredit or dispose of others with a difference of opinion is fruitless, and a waste of time, energy, and effort. We must behave like mature adults, not children seeking attention and adoration. I have tried to come up with a name for our movement and have struggled and discarded several. But one name keeps popping up --*The Changers*.

There may be a much better one, but whatever it is, our movement's name must be something different because *we* are different. We are not racist, ultra-liberal, extreme right-wingers, or socialists. We believe in freedom of almost everything – we are *The Changers.*

After reading this book, you may feel somewhat depressed, insecure and unconfident. But we are entering a new, exciting, and innovative era, and we must embrace it, contribute to it, improve upon it, and strive aggressively to make it better. I am impressed and amazed at the young students I encounter in graduate education, as well as those with recent professional or graduate degrees. Their knowledge, energy, and commitment are encouraging and exciting. They are much more knowledgeable and advanced compared to my status at that stage.

We are on a threshold of change. It can be a cliff ending in a valley of doom, or riding a beautiful rainbow to a bountiful and fulfilling future. I doubt there is a middle ground. I think that within a few centuries, we will either have become extinct, or we will be living a better and longer life, probably with an average lifespan of over 100 years. To accomplish the better of the two outcomes will not be easy or effortless, but the rewards will be remarkable. We must protect not only our future and destiny but that of millions of other species before moving on to those that are less urgent. Unless we make significant changes, I believe that 50 million years from now, some other advanced species will be searching for our fossils and trying to determine what we were, who we were, and why we disappeared.

This could be the beginning of a great new era, and it is our responsibility to push forward and disseminate that information. The younger generation is the future. I hope they do the right thing and become the nation's leaders. We need a new generation of informed and dedicated leaders, and I urge all of you to become an active part of *The Changers*.

Thank you for reading this book. I wish you a lengthy, prosperous, and rewarding life.

H. Lewis Smith
H. Lewis Smith
jackbiz1145@gmail.com

ABOUT THE AUTHOR

H. Lewis Smith, M.D., is a retired surgeon who lives in Southern California with his wife of 33 years. He was born in a small east Texas town where his father owned a modest cattle ranch. He is deeply grateful to his first-grade teacher, who recognized his intellectual talent and encouraged him to pursue higher education. He also gives great credit to his mother, who always supported his dreams.

Dr. Smith received his medical degree from the University of Tennessee and served his residency in surgery at Staten Island, New York. After establishing a private practice in Whittier, CA, he later became the chief of staff of Whittier Hospital Medical Center. As the father of five children and stepfather to two, Dr. Smith has known the heights of joy in being a father and mentor. He has also endured the sorrow caused by the deaths of three of his children.

A previous avid and accomplished fisherman, Dr. Smith has turned his attention to writing as a second career in his retirement and is the author of four additional acclaimed books.

Long interested in national politics, he was invited to attend the second inauguration of Richard M. Nixon, whose brother had been his patient. Dr. Smith's political leanings are neither Republican nor Democratic. He has combined the thinking of many political entities into a comprehensive view of the strengths and weaknesses of modern politics. He has thus developed a nonpartisan vision for crucial improvements, which he incisively examines in *The Big Crunch and the Fix*.